FRENCH BULLDOG

Coloring Book

For Adults & Kids

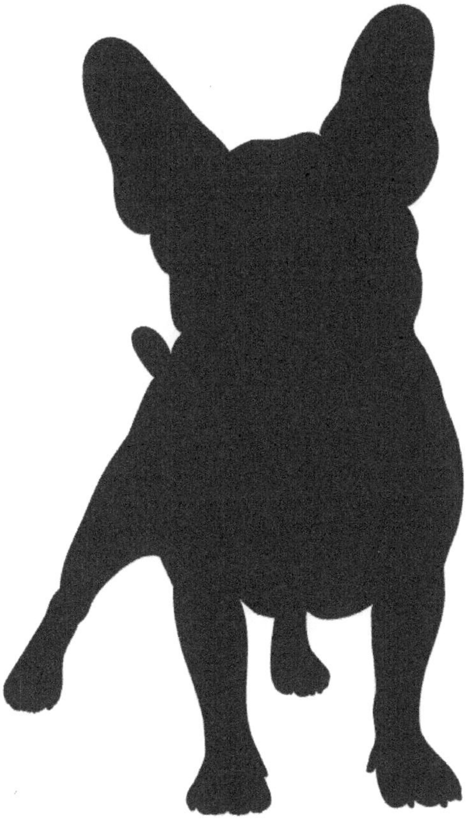

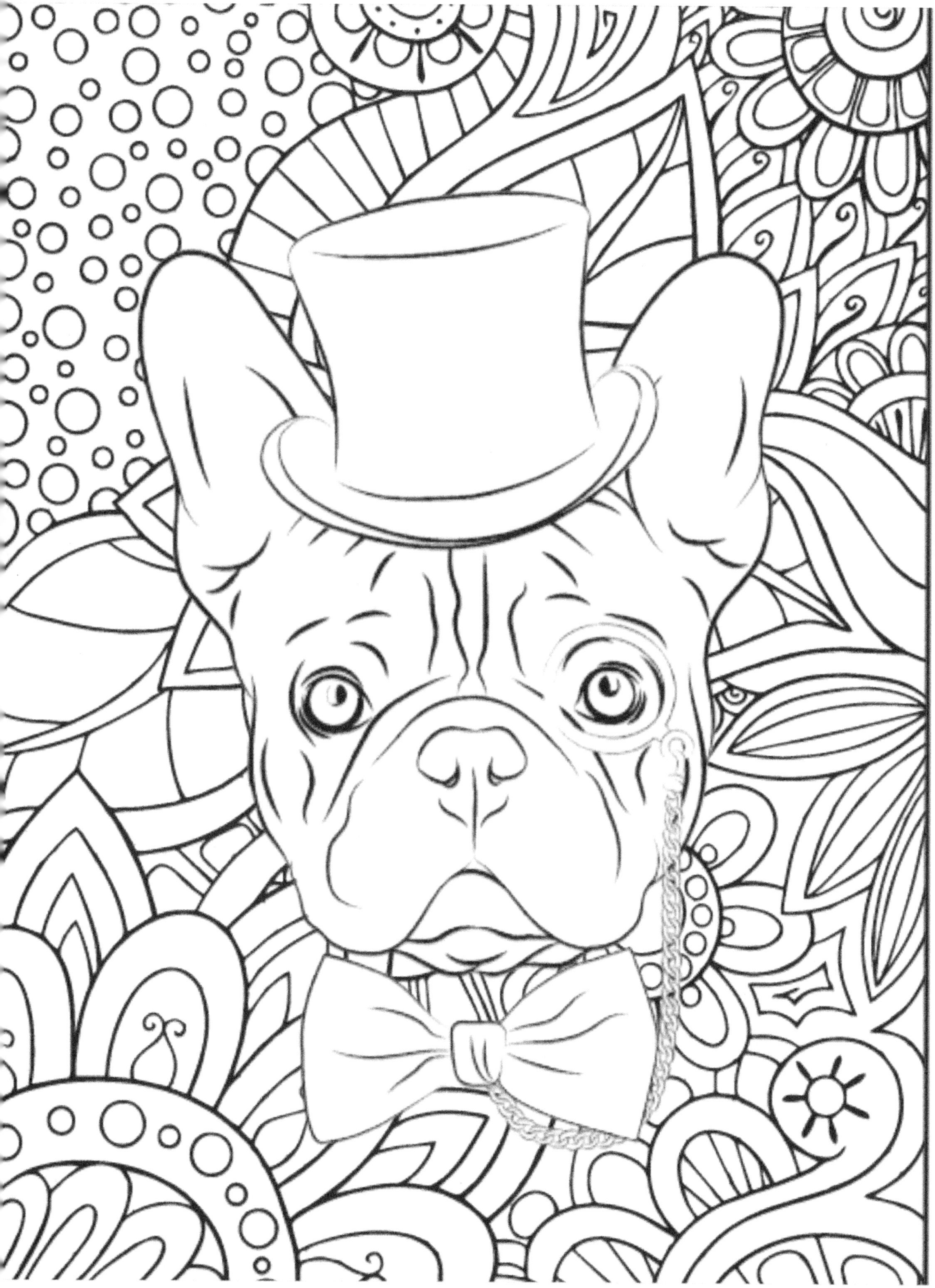

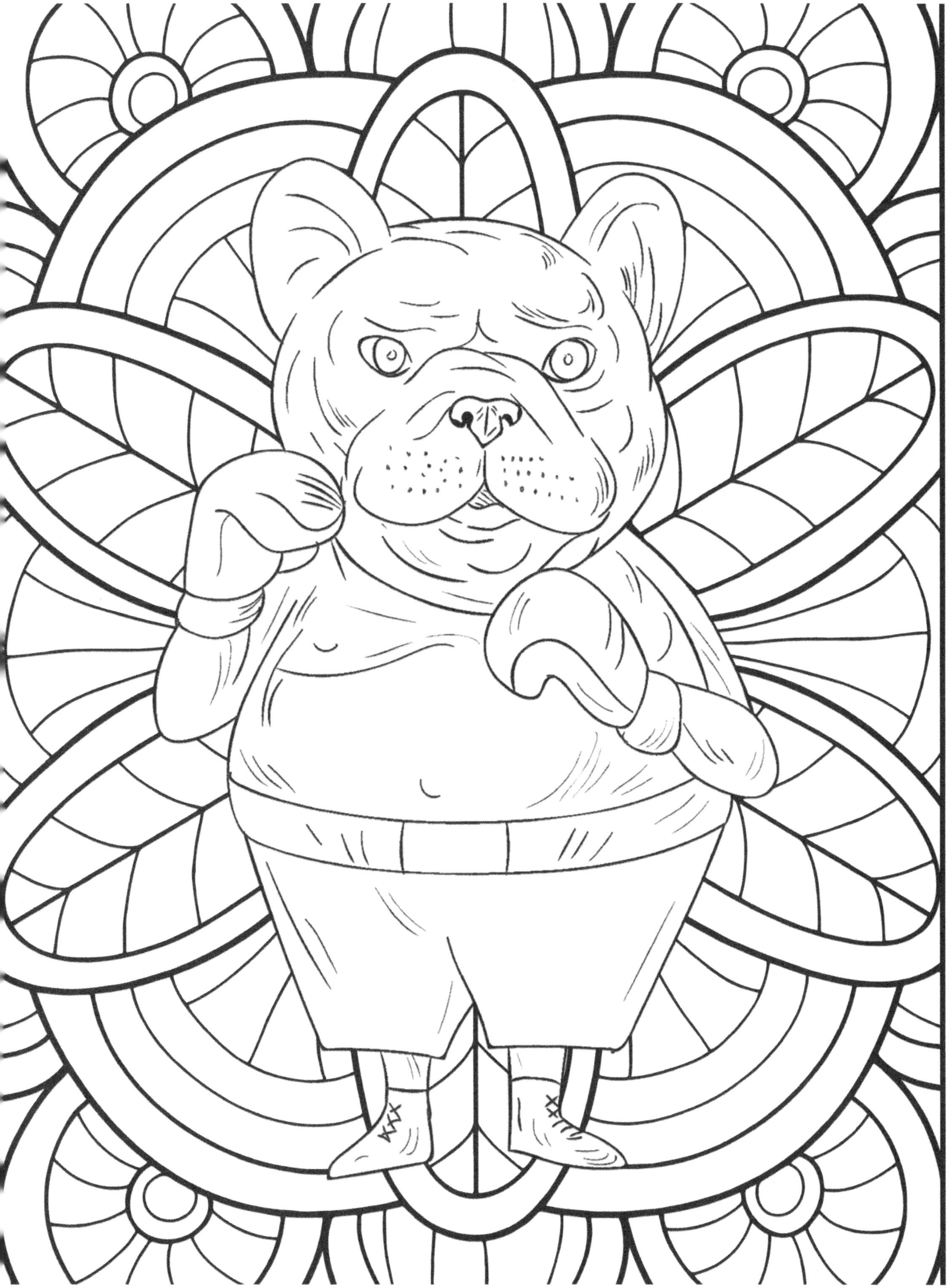

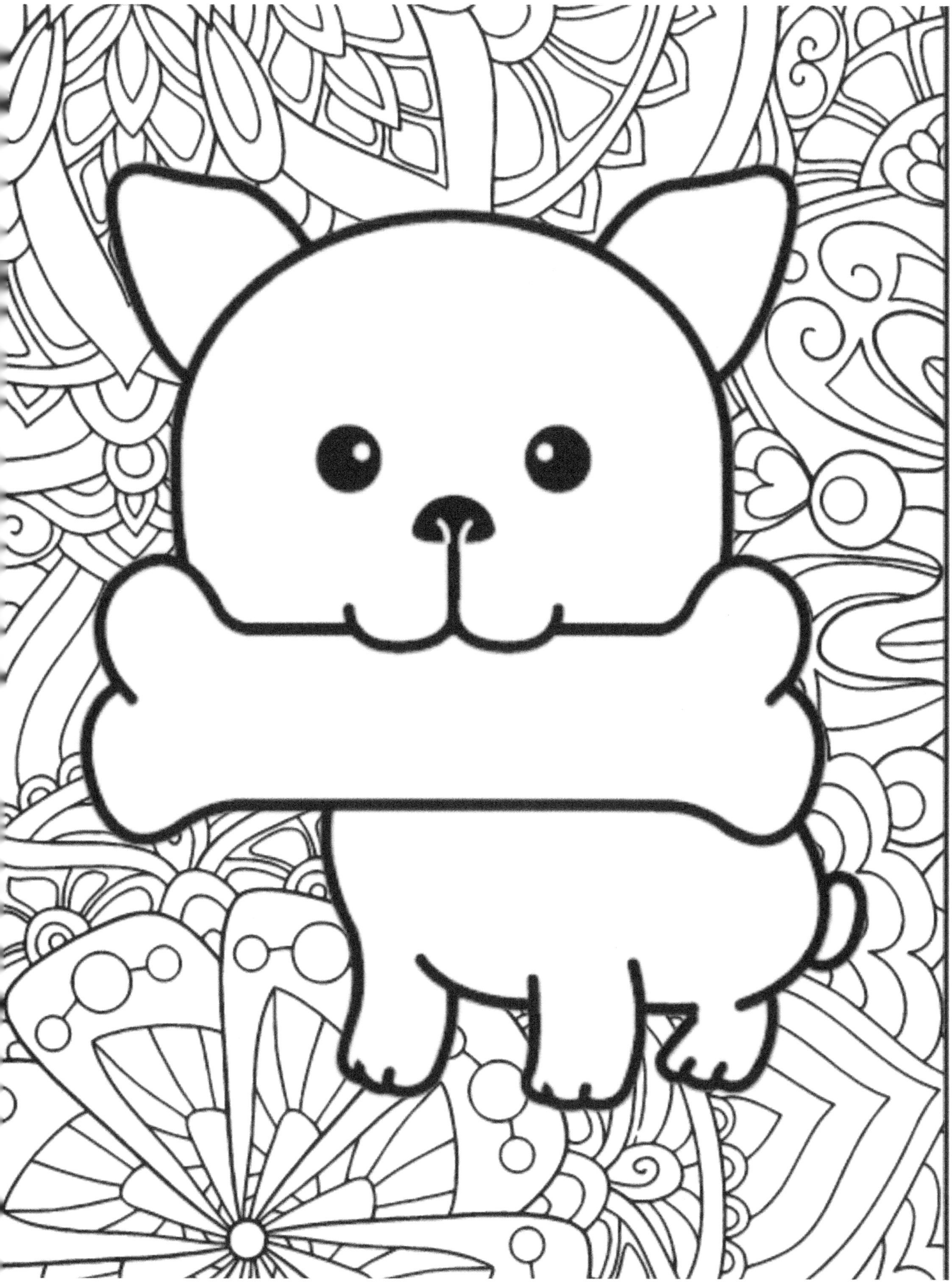

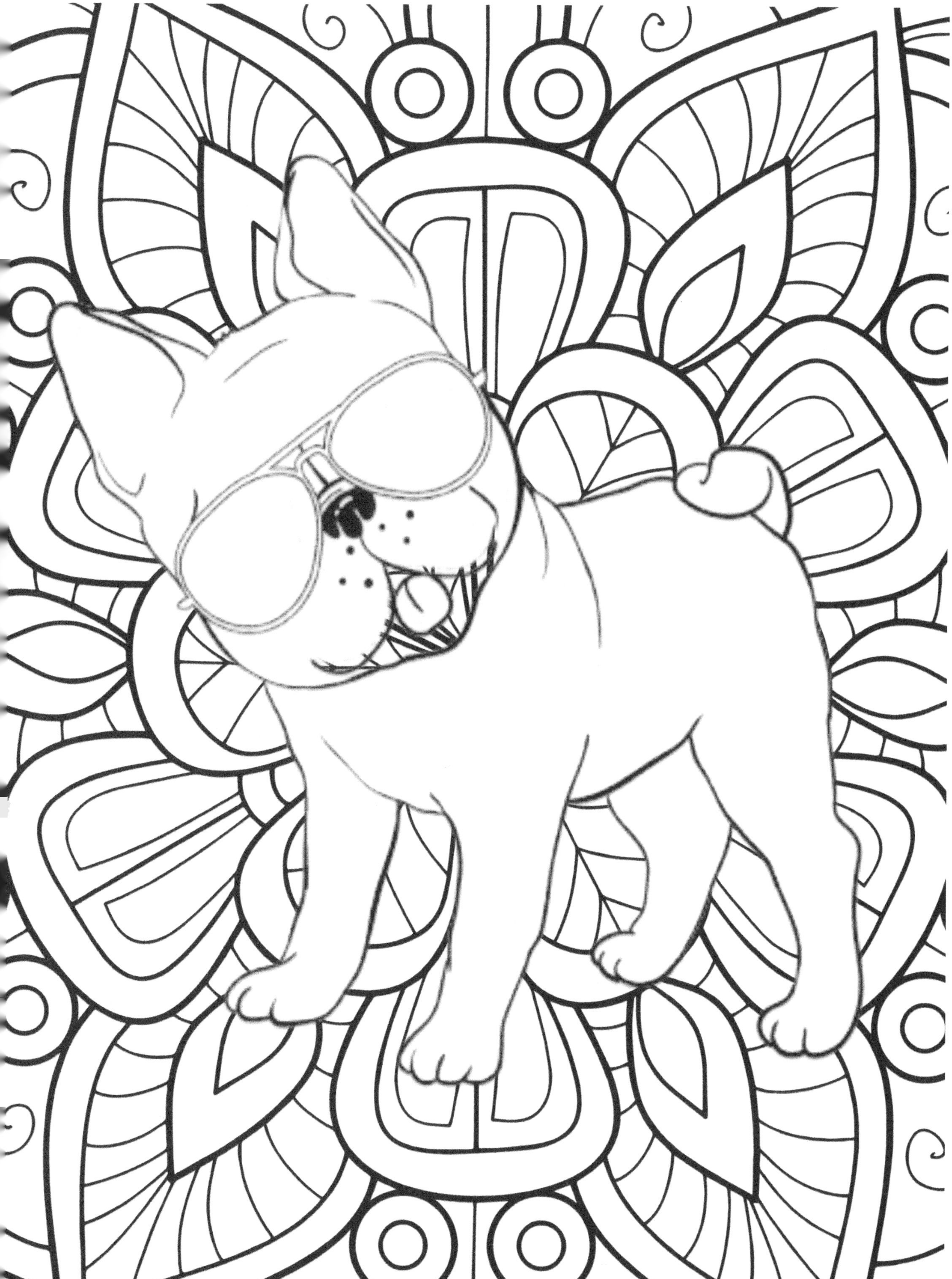

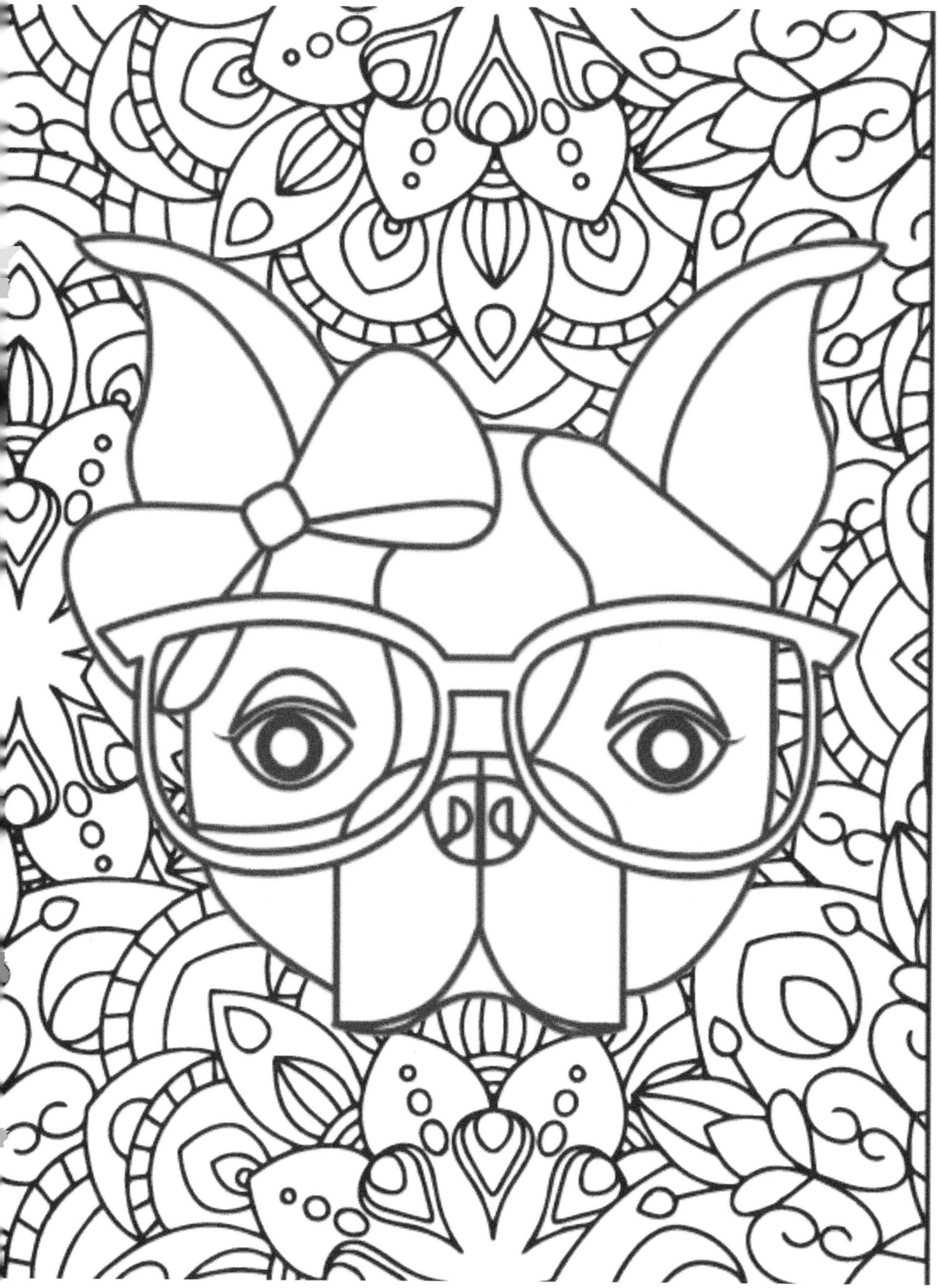

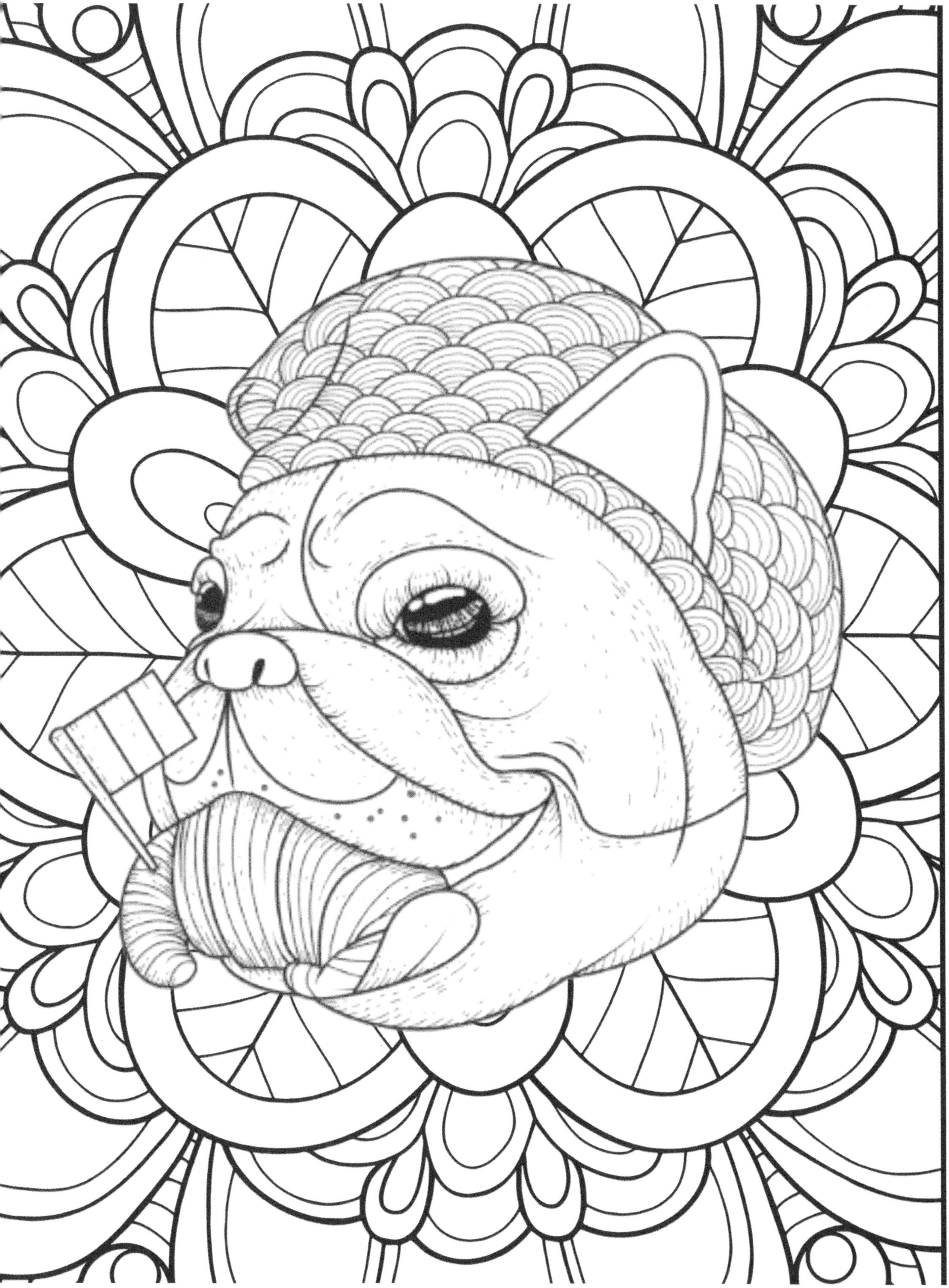

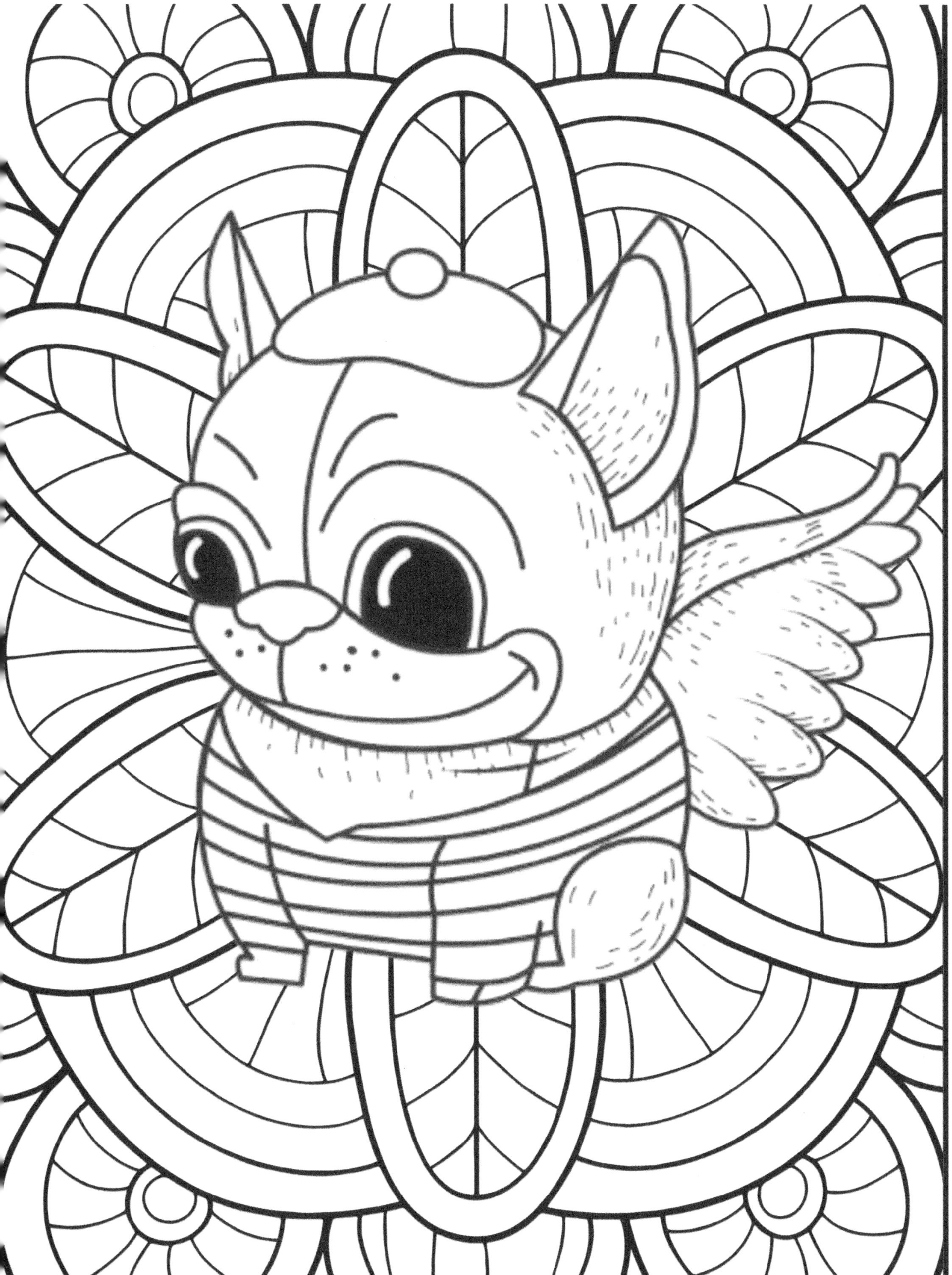

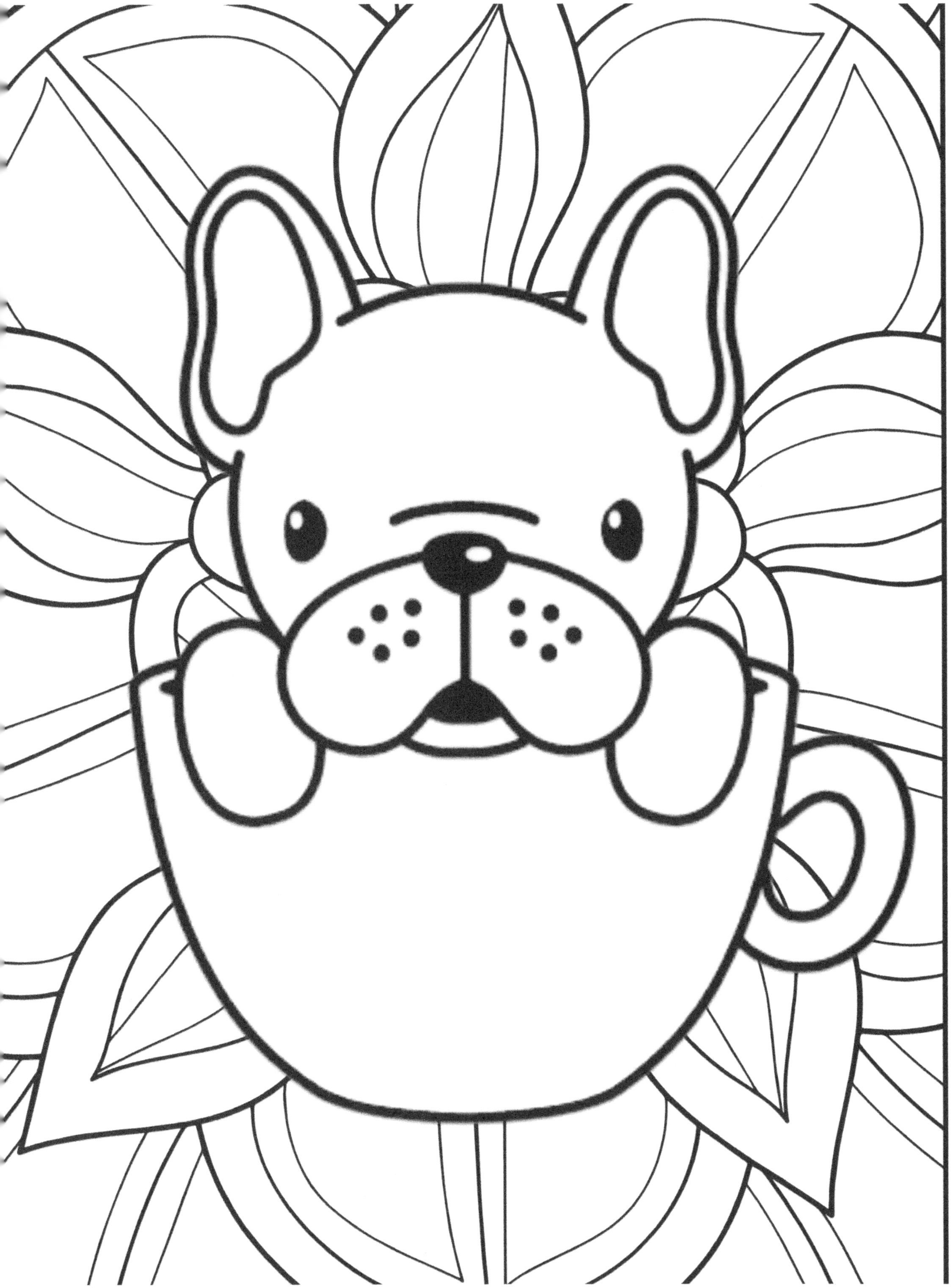

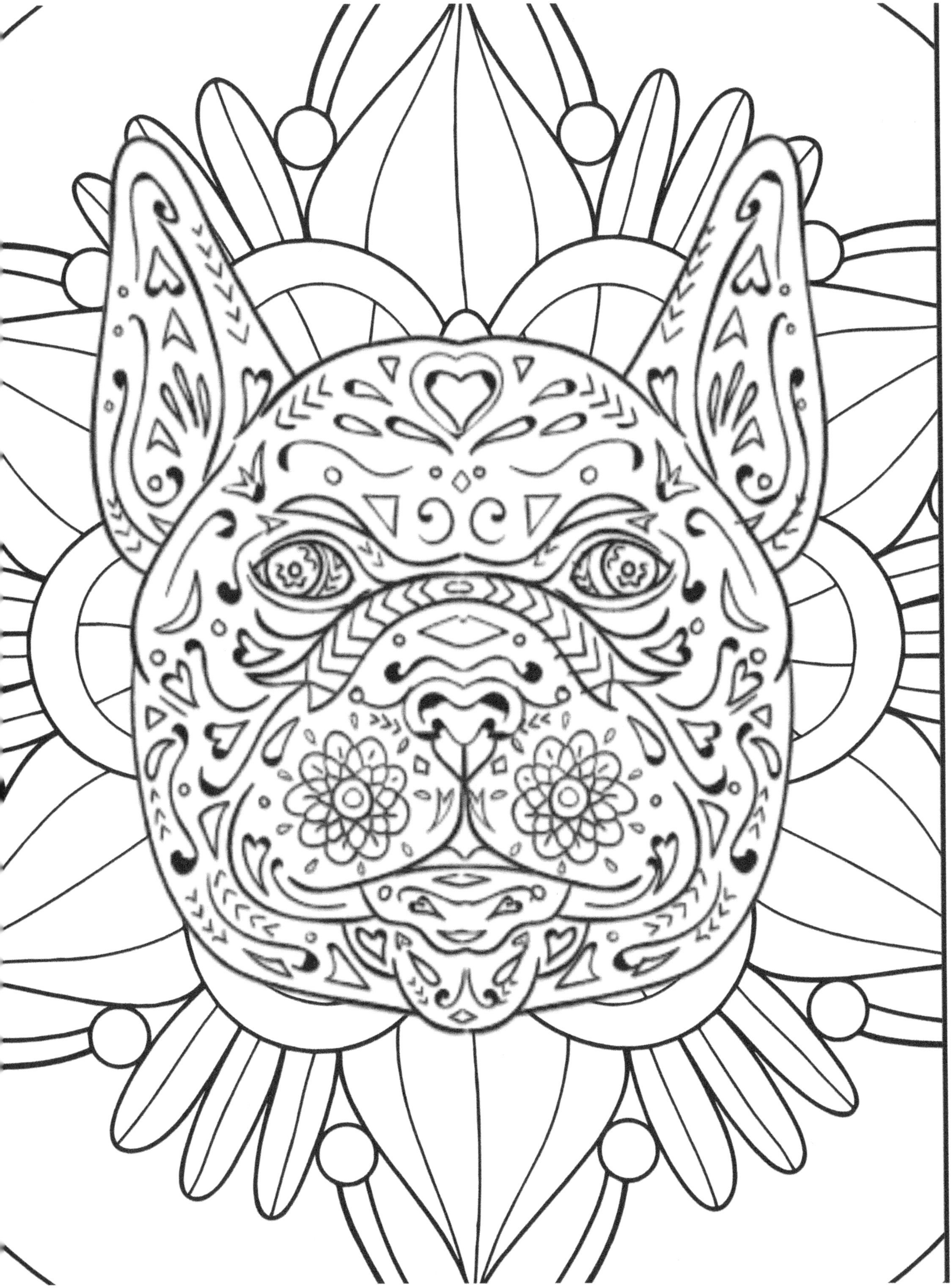

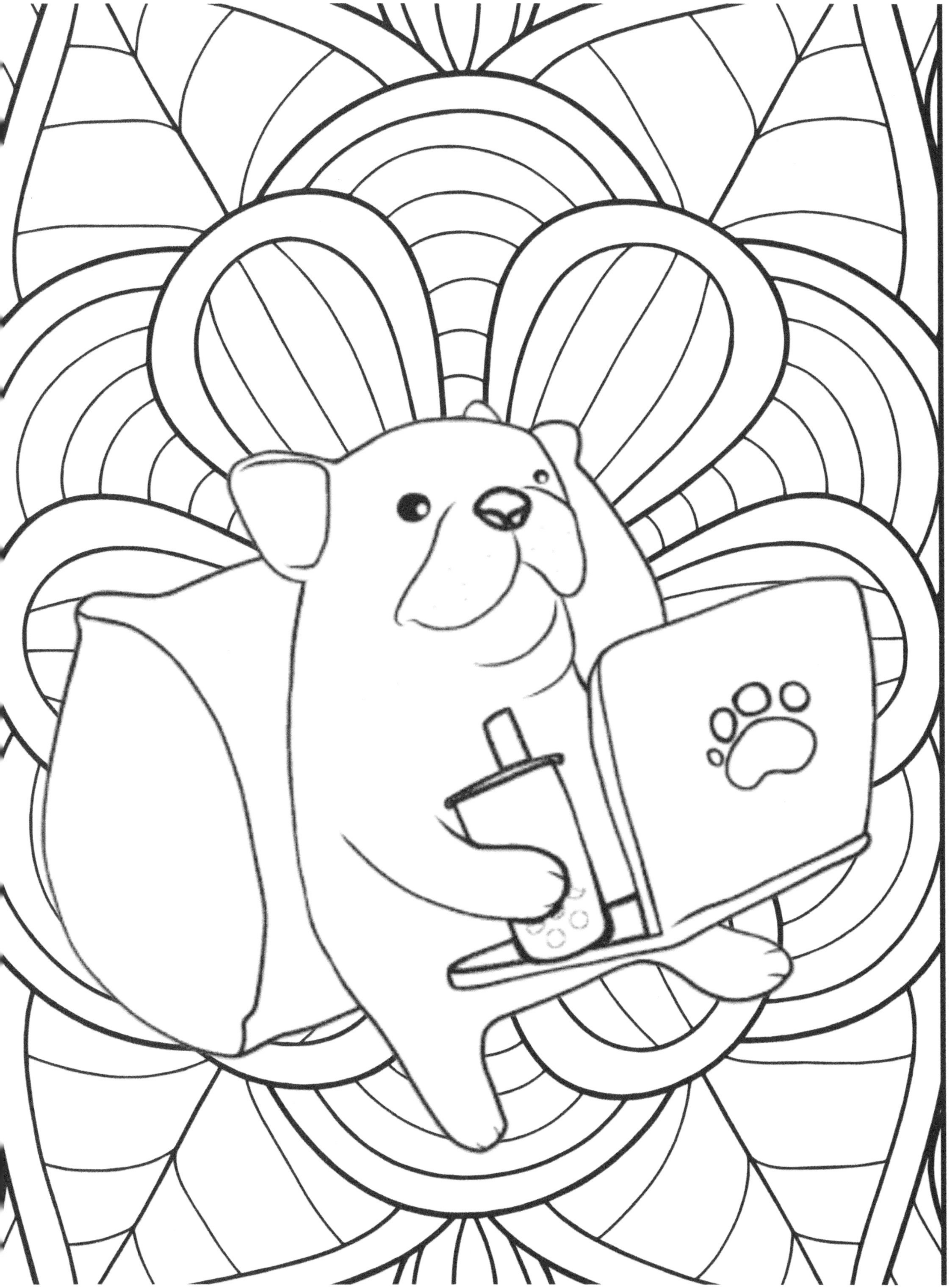

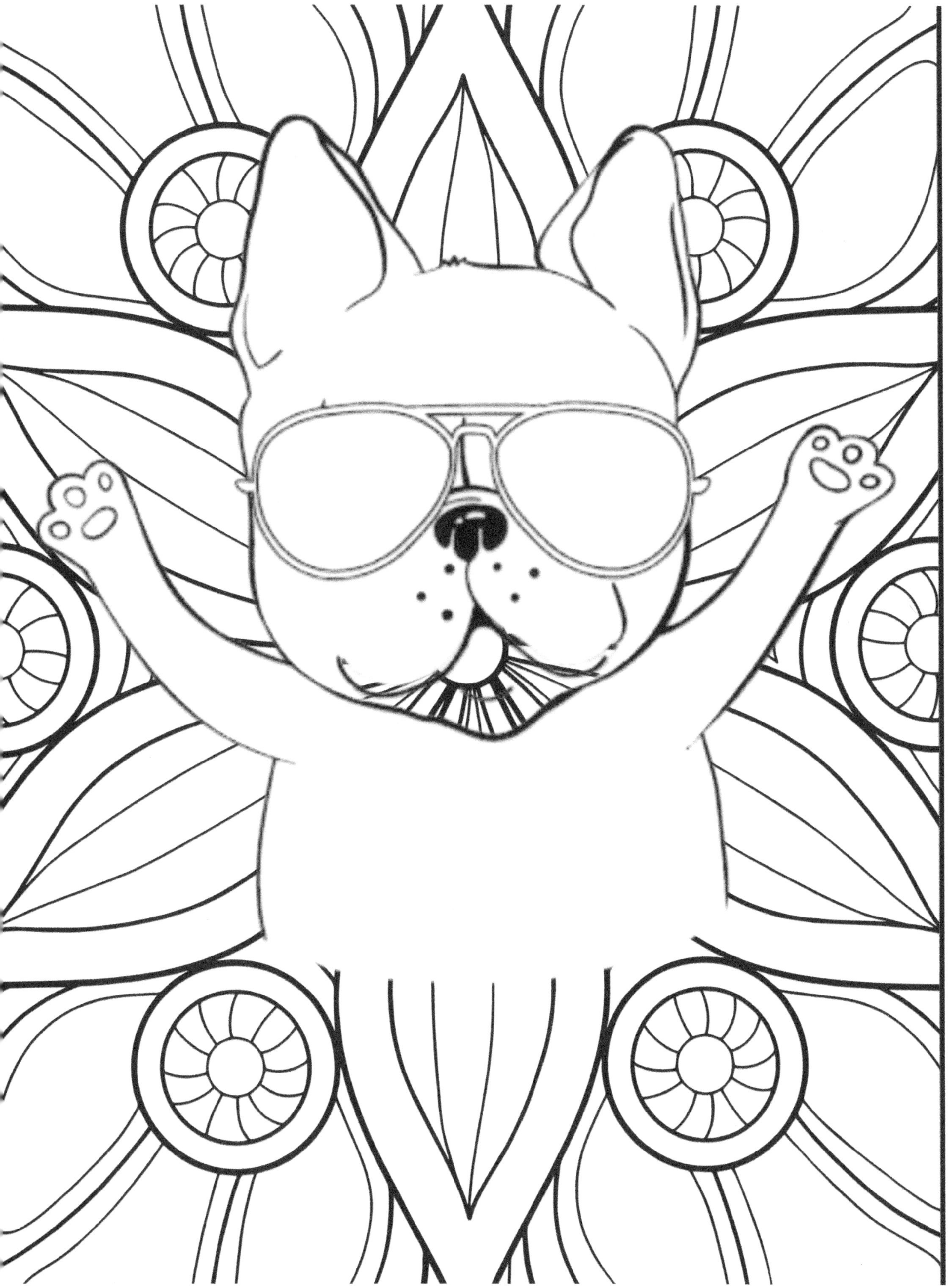

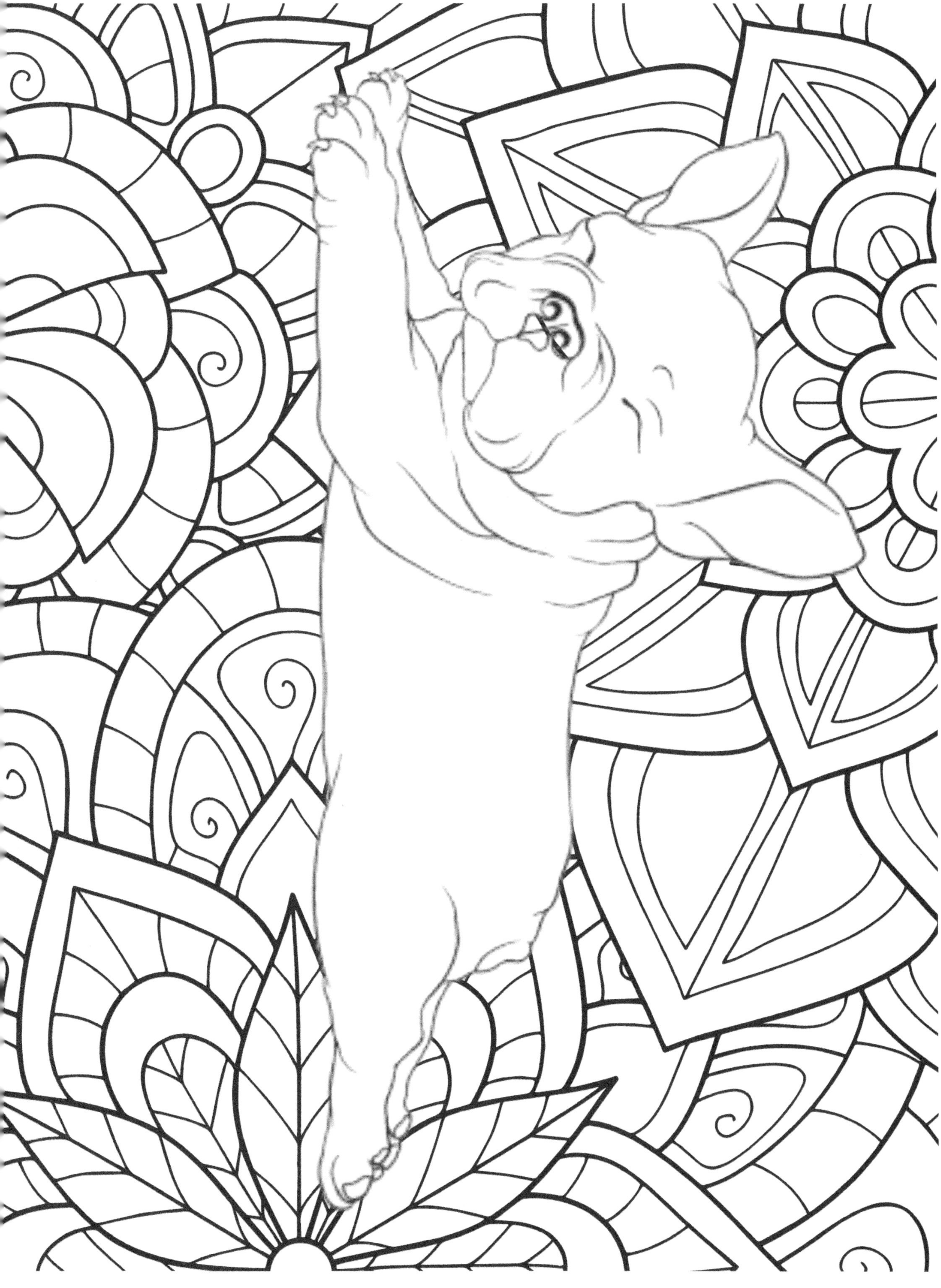

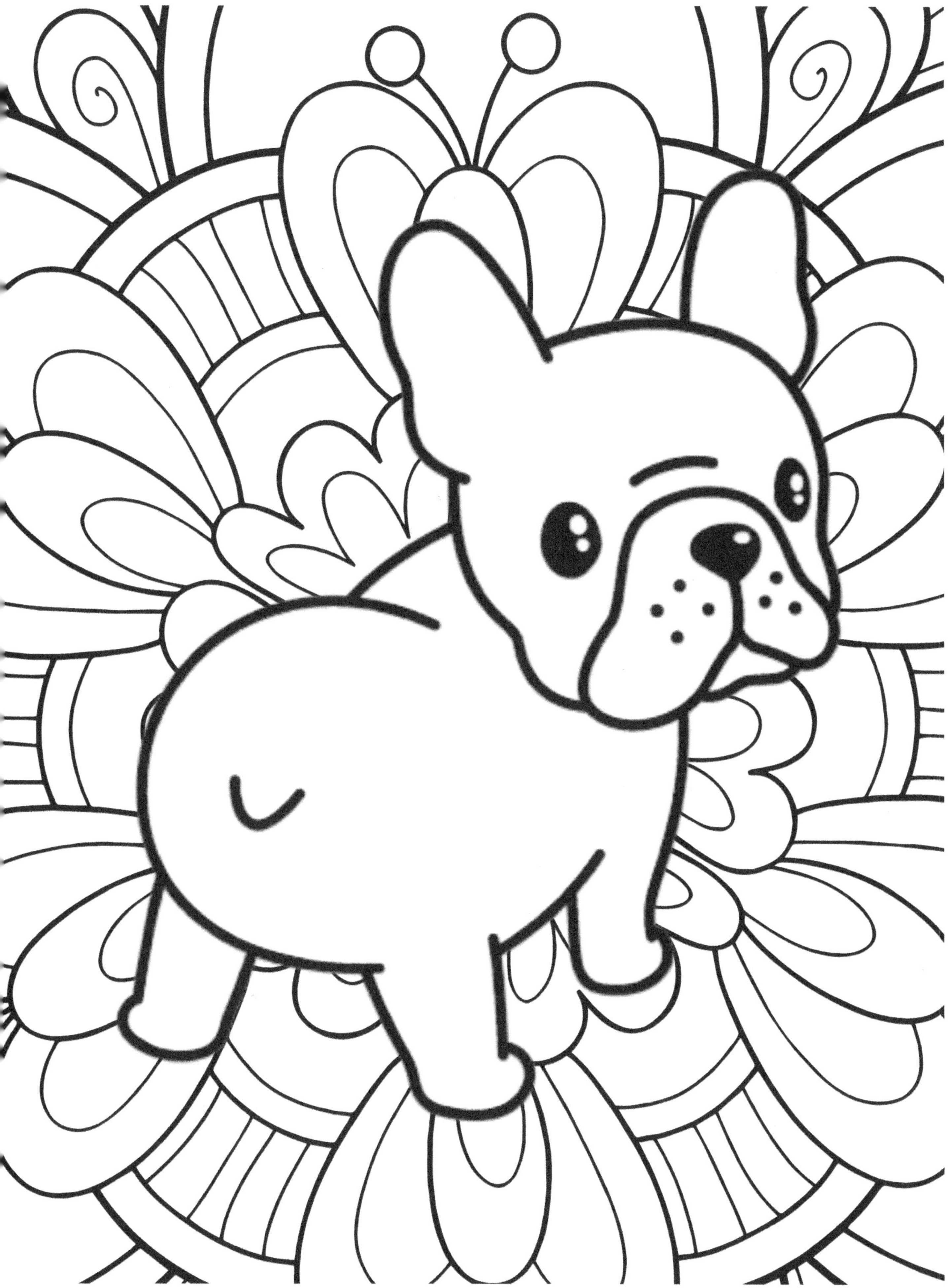

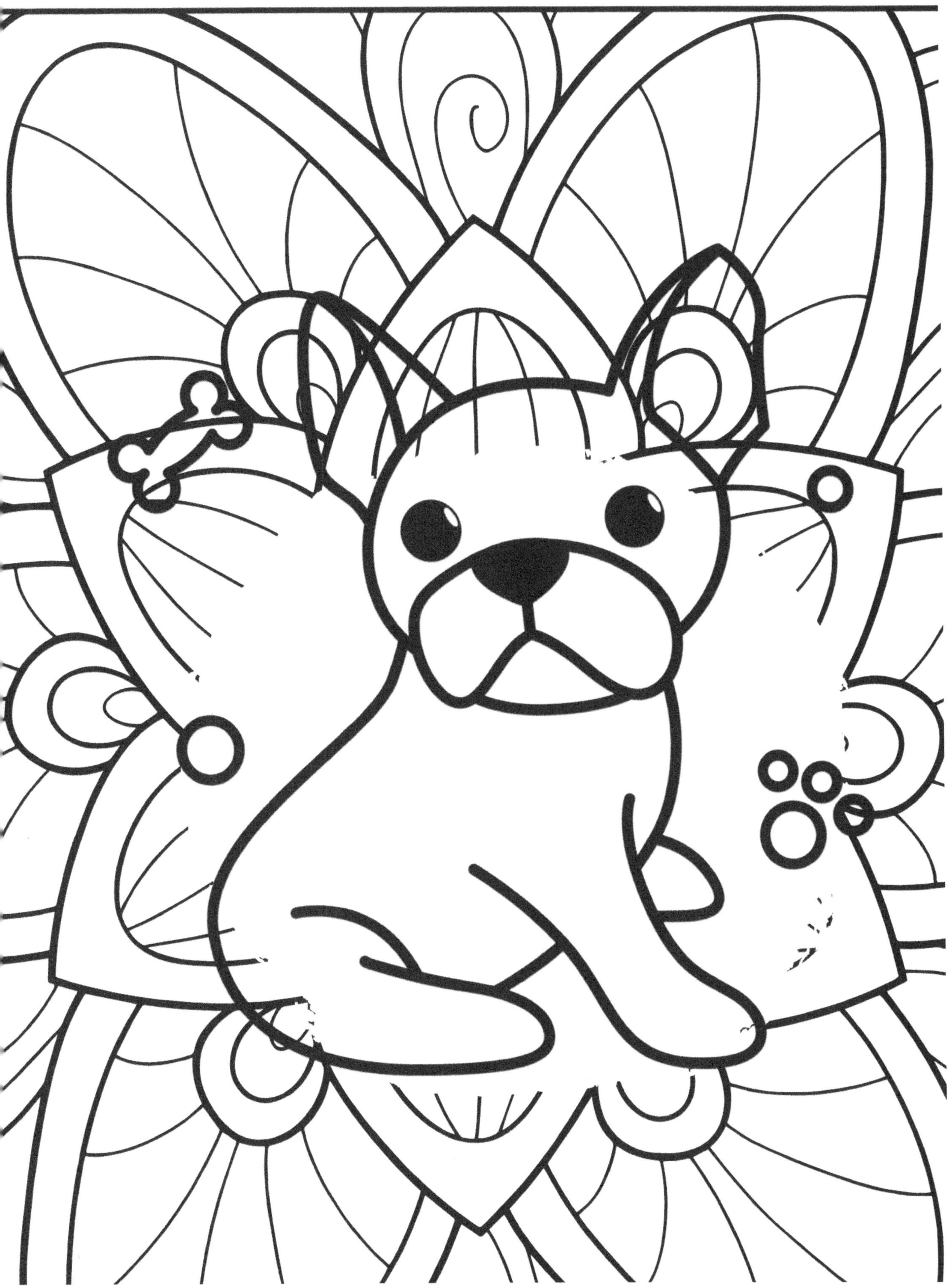

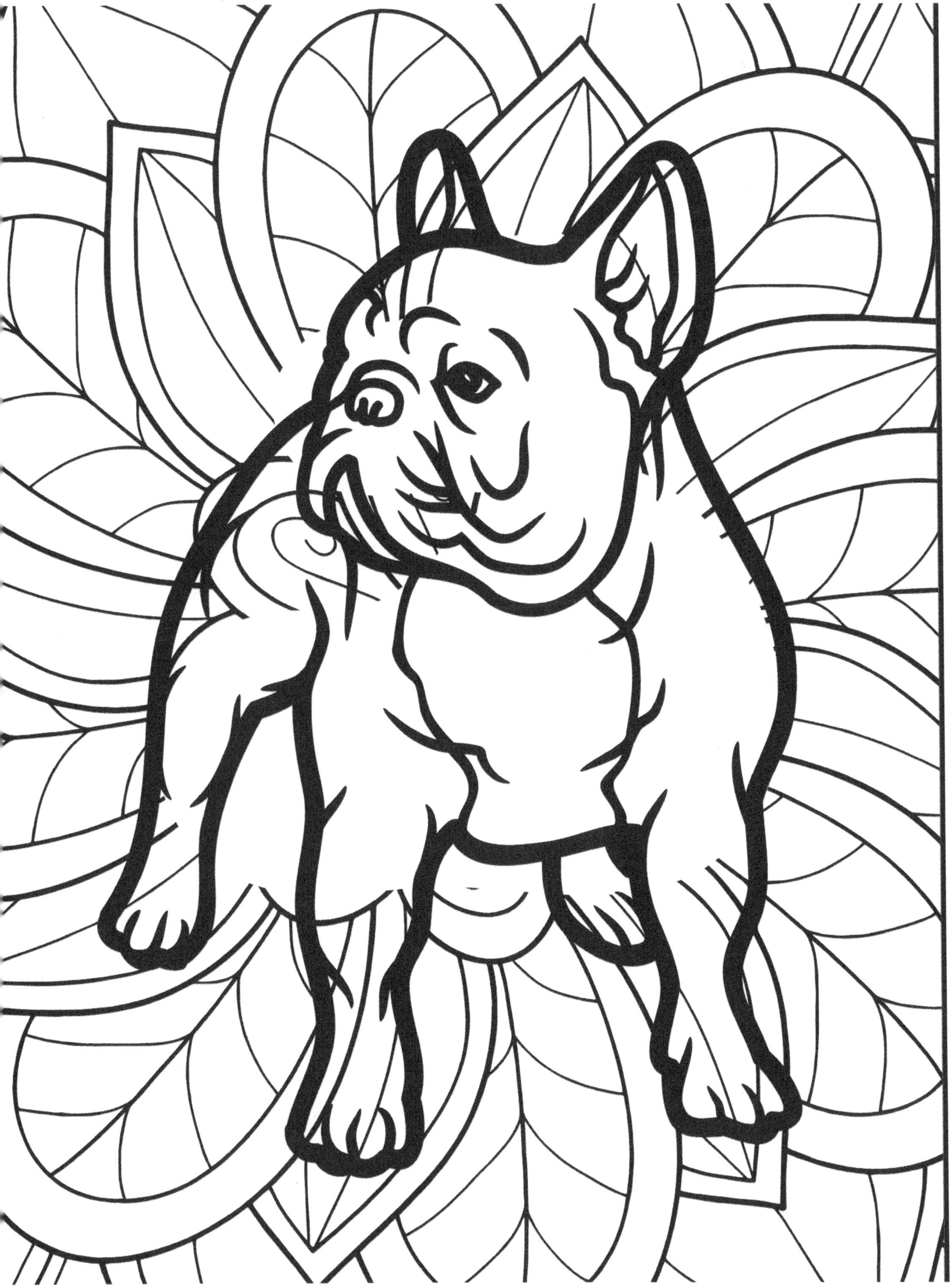

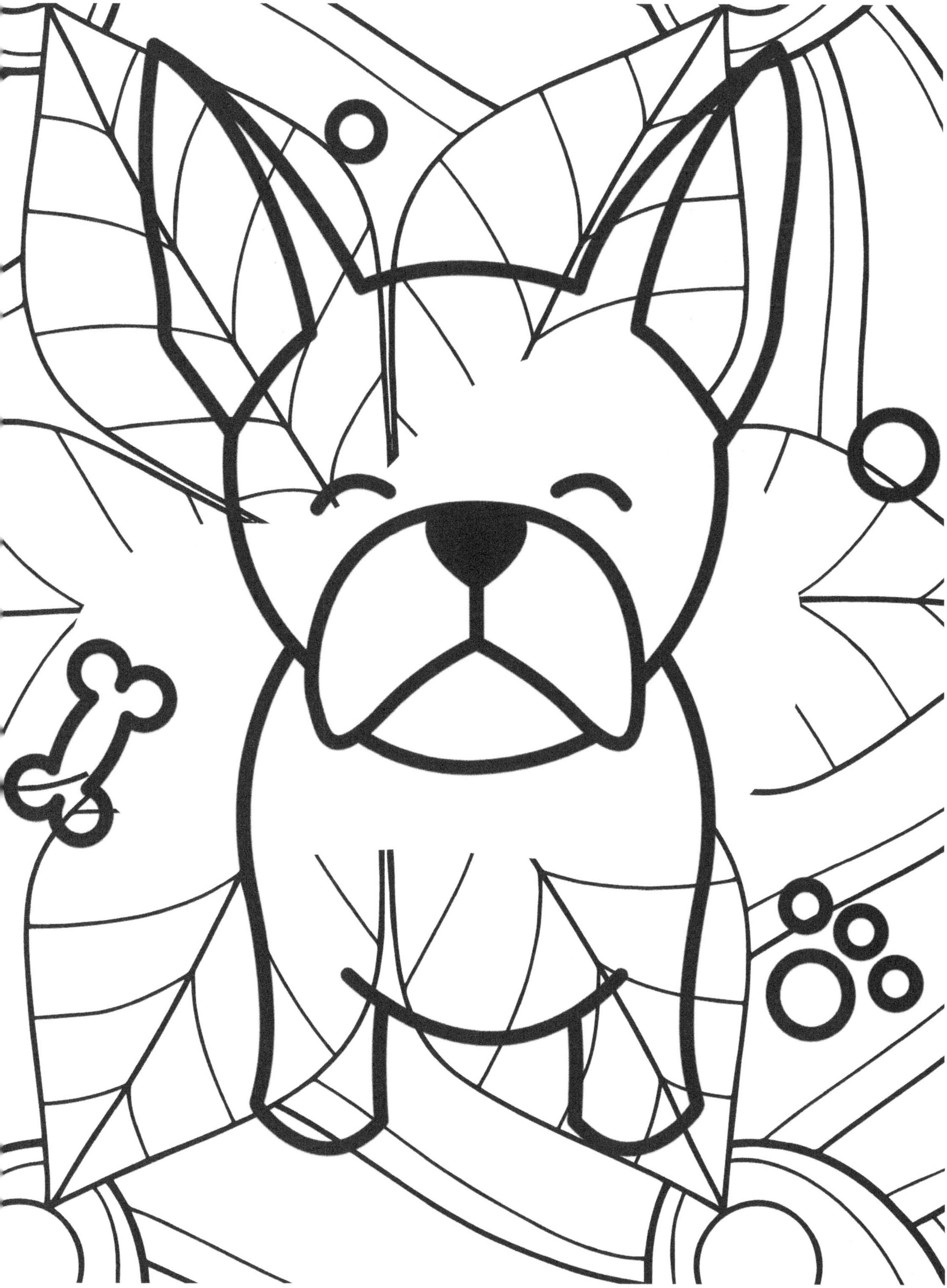

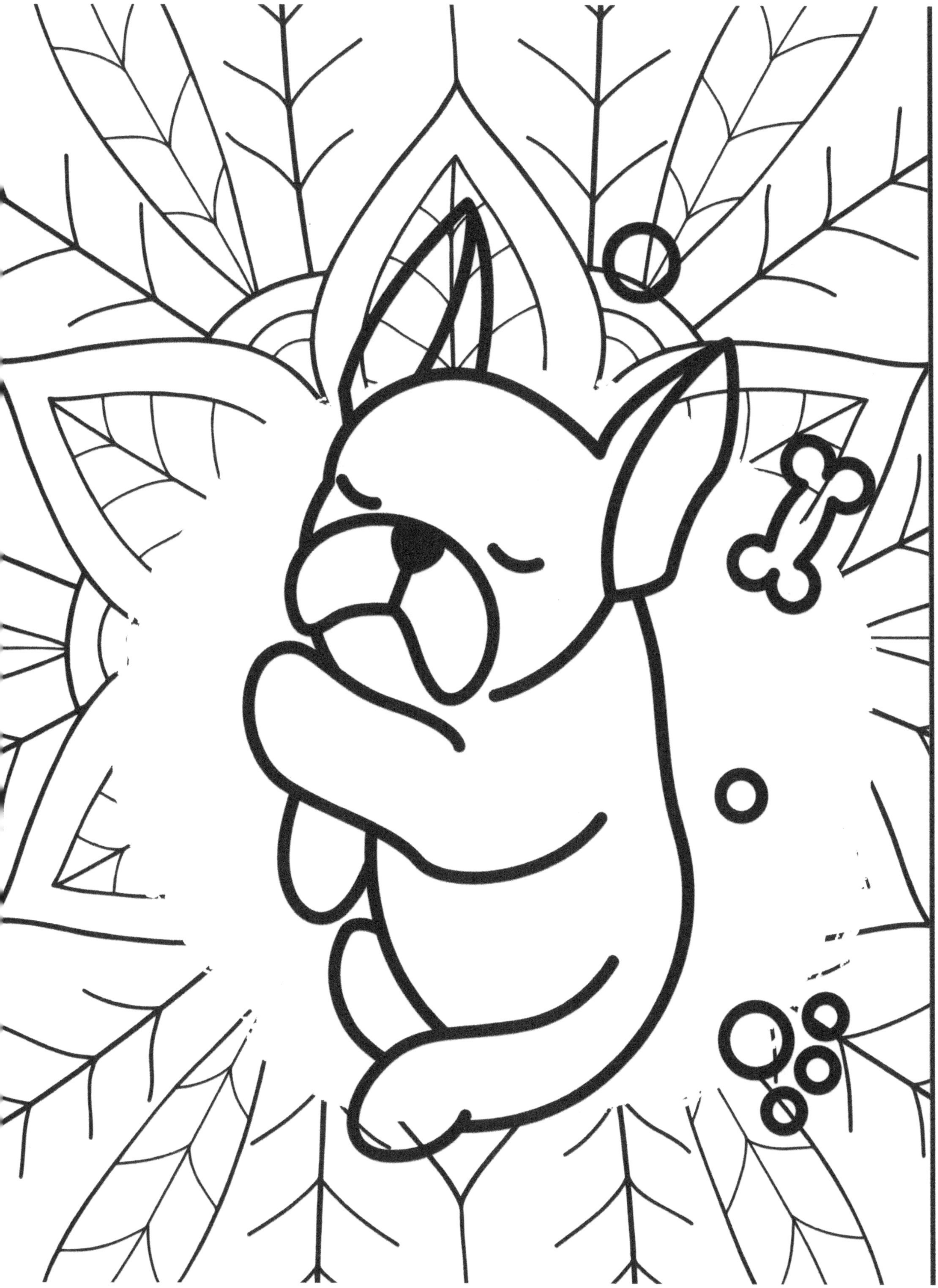

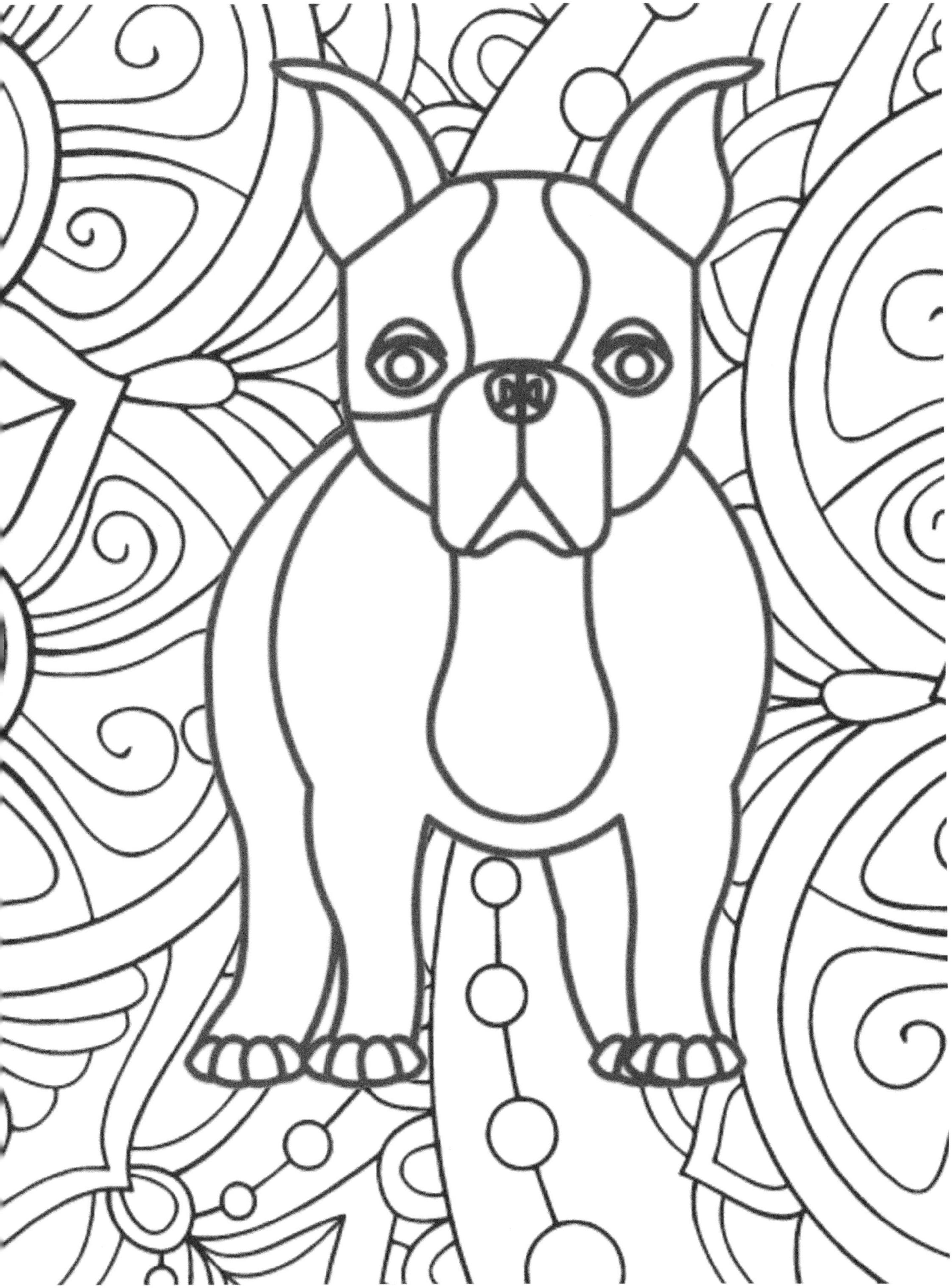

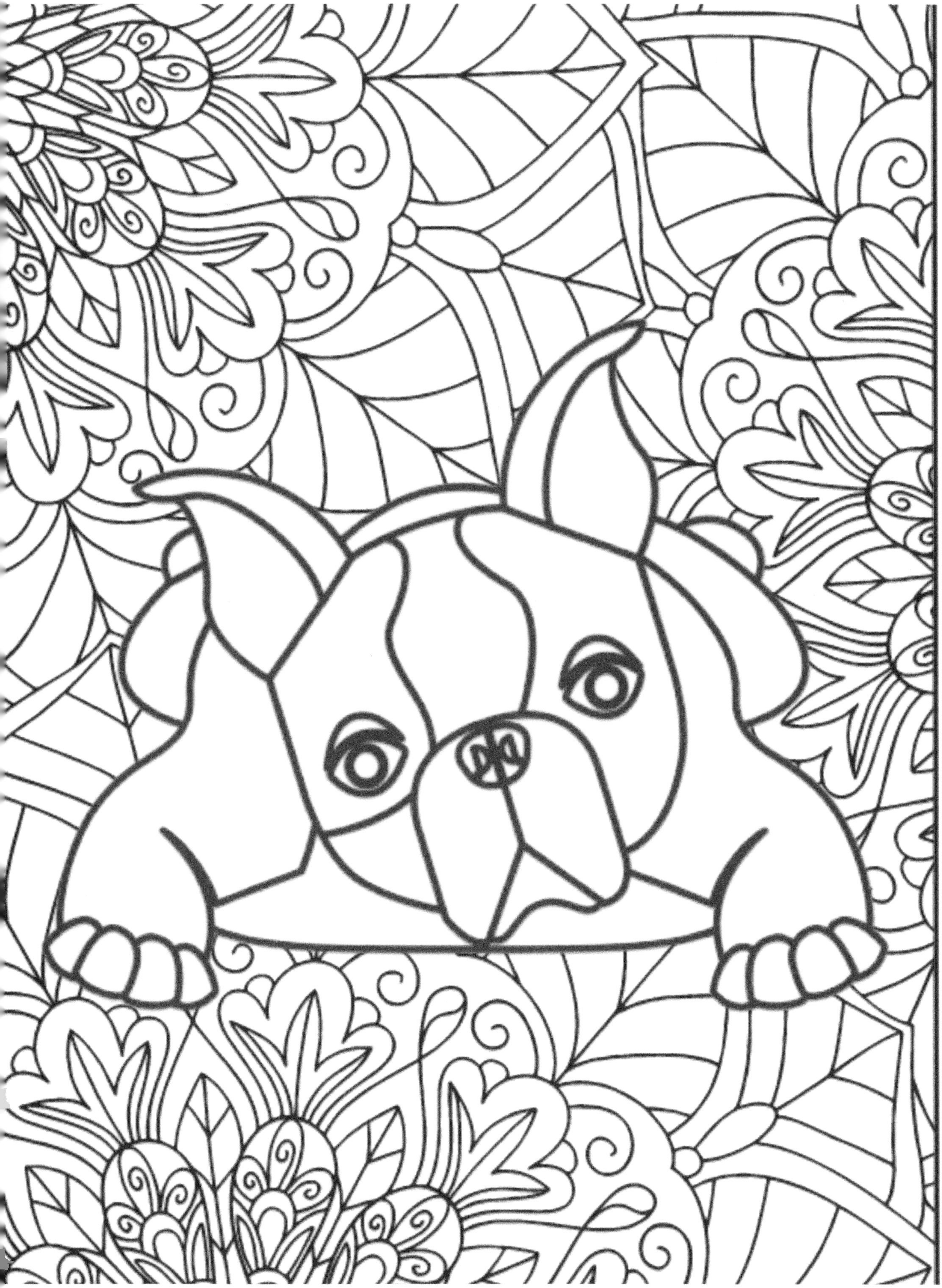

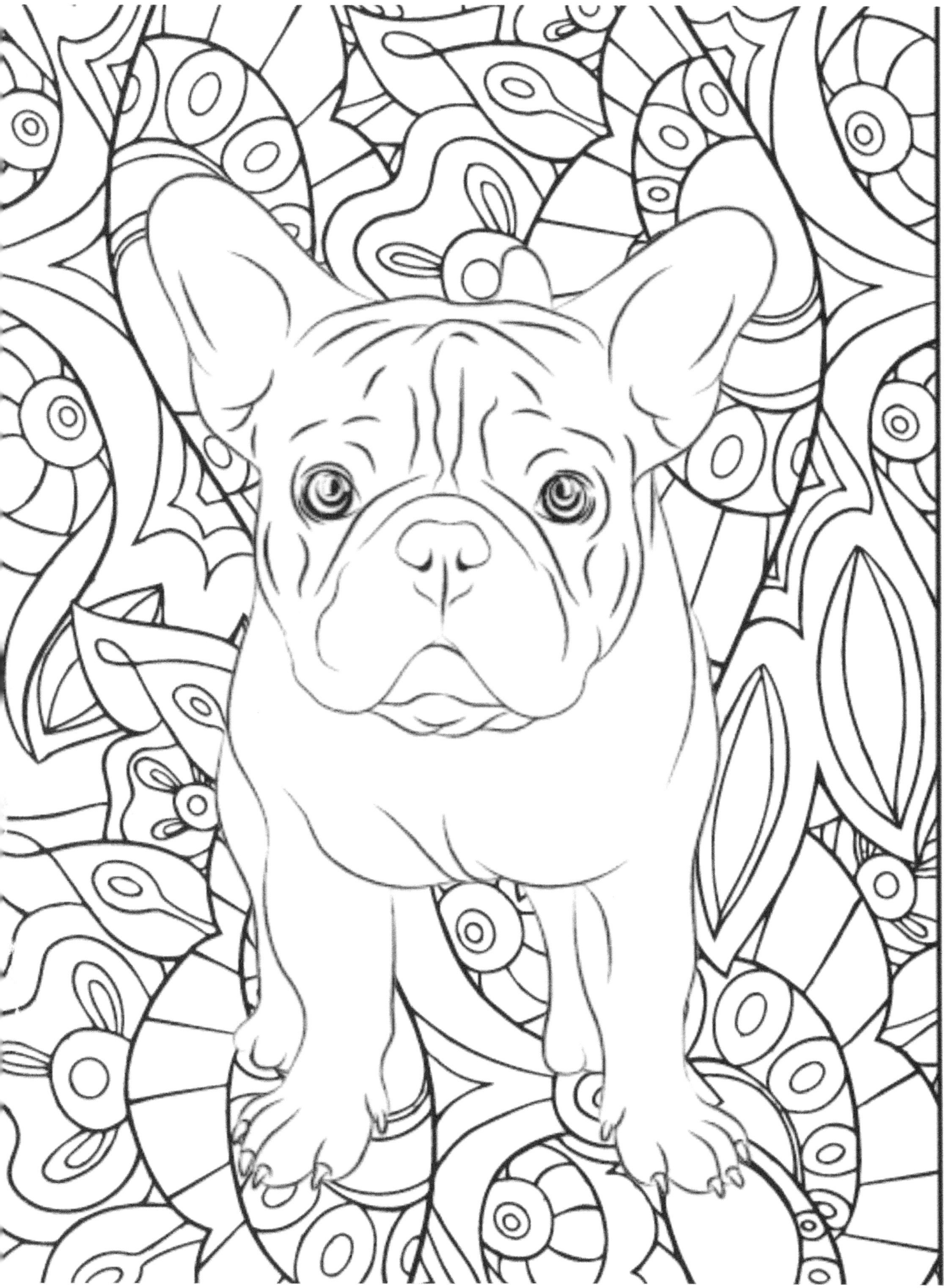

Made in United States
North Haven, CT
30 December 2024

63758705R00024